BODACIOUS

BODACIOUS

Controversial and Provocative

NATHANIEL SHORT

J Merrill Publishing, Inc., Columbus 43207
www.JMerrill.pub

Copyright © 2021 J Merrill Publishing, Inc.
All rights reserved. No part of this publication may be reproduced, distributed, or transmitted in any form or by any means, including photocopying, recording, or other electronic or mechanical methods, without the prior written permission of the publisher, except in the case of brief quotations embodied in critical reviews and certain other noncommercial uses permitted by copyright law. For permission requests, contact J Merrill Publishing, Inc., 434 Hillpine Drive, Columbus, OH 43207
Published 2021

All scriptures in this book are quoted from the Holy Bible containing the Old and New Testaments translated out of the original tongues, conformable to the edition of 1611, commonly known as the authorized or King James Version.

Library of Congress Control Number: 2021910435
ISBN-13: 978-1-954414-04-4 (Paperback)
ISBN-13: 978-1-954414-03-7 (eBook)

Title: Bodacious: Controversial and Provocative
Author: Nathaniel Short

This book is dedicated to my family.

Thanks for all the love.

bo-da-cious [boh-dey-shuhs]

- Adjective originating from South Midland and Southern United States.

1. Through; blatant; unmistakable
2. Remarkable; outstanding
3. Audacious; bold or brazen

CONTENTS

Introduction   xi

1. Tithe or Not to Tithe?   1
2. The Law   35
3. Grace or Disgrace   45
4. Will a Man Rob God?   55
   Epilogue   59

INTRODUCTION

Bodacious is a word that intrigued me. Once I learned the definition, I thought it would be a good title for my book. I wanted one bold word.

After several attempts to understand why the church tithes, the answer conflicted with my belief that we are no longer under the law of tithes. Being rebuked by pastors and elders of the church and experiencing the informality of being excommunicated, I didn't want to disrupt the congregation or argue the Bible and become the author of confusion. So after much prayer, fasting, and studying the word of God, my research on the subject of tithing was a conformation that affirmed with solemnity the dignity and seriousness of my belief about tithing.

As a young minister on fire for God, it hurt me to go to church and hear the big dogs preach untruths, and the flock takes it as gospel. This inspired me to express my thoughts in writing with a comprehensive list of scriptures. I am not the authoritative source, but I find my opinion appropriate, especially in this era of fake news and alternative facts.

At first, I needed to be right about this subject, but God removed that need from my spirit when a wise woman (Sister Robin Jackson) told me that God gave you this opinion. He didn't give it to everybody! That lead me to believe the interpretation of scripture is between each individual and God.

All I have to do is plant the seed of my thoughts, 5 percent of the work. God's word will convict and do the other 95 percent. Therefore, I write to share my opinion, as a modern-day reformer like those of the Reformation of the 16th-century movement in Western Europe for the reform of The

Roman Catholic Church, which resulted in the Protestant Church's establishment.

I am not a Theologian, but may my works and actions enlighten the Babes in Christ, challenge the status quo, both now and in times to come. "What you leave behind is not what is engraved in stone monuments, but what is woven into the lives of others."

May this book be the legacy of my spiritual journey, woven into the hearts and minds of Kingdom builders.

CHAPTER 1
TITHE OR NOT TO TITHE?

Tithe. A tenth part, or 10 percent, given as a tribute for religious purposes.

Two instances before the setting up of The Law Covenant in which tithes were given. Abraham gave Melchizedek one-tenth of the spoils of his victory over Chedorlaomer (Genesis 14:18-20). Jacob vowed at Bethel to give one-tenth of his substance to God (Genesis 28:20- 22). These two accounts are merely instances of voluntarily giving one-tenth and recognized as a holy deed. There is no record to the effect that Abraham or Jacob commanded their descendants to follow such examples, thereby establishing a religious practice, custom, or law. There was no law or custom to tithe until the inauguration of the law covenant, not before.

Mosaic tithing laws were established to support Israel's temple and priesthood; the obligation to pay tithes would cease when The Mosaic Law Covenant came to an end as fulfilled through Christ's death on the cross. Having abolished in His flesh the enmity, even the Law of the Commandments contained in ordinances (Ephesians 2:15). Abolish means "to reduce to inactivity." God has abolished all ordinances, rule, authority, and power of the law rendering them inactive. They are of no effect after their temporary use was fulfilled. The believer has been discharged from the law. *And you, being dead in your sins and the 1, circumcision of your flesh, hath he quickened together with him, having forgiven you all trespasses; blotting out the handwriting of ordinances that was against us which was contrary to us, and took it out of the way, nailing it to His cross (Colossians 2:13-14).* Spiritual reality is not found in legalism but in Christ's blood that canceled the written code because we could not meet the demands. For this reason, the law was "against us."

Our inability to fulfill the obligation of obedience to the Mosaic Law was a death sentence that was graciously blotted out. We are free of the bill of indictment and quickened to a new spiritual life. For sin shall not have dominion over you; for ye are not under the law but under grace (Romans 6:14). As believers, we exercise our faith in Christ and the spirit's law of grace. The authoritative rule of conduct for the New Testament church is humble obedience to grace, which includes the eternal Moral Law embodied in the Mosaic Law but excludes the ceremonial regulations that are procedural and substitutes works for faith. For the Law of the Spirit of Life in Christ Jesus hath made me free from the Law of Sin and Death (Romans 8:2).

The universal principle of the Law of the Spirit of Life in Christ Jesus is that He, the indwelling Holy Spirit, enables believers to dominate the law of Sin and Death. Our obligation to Christ empowers us even over death. We are no longer spiritually dead being apart from the Law of Moses. But if ye be led of the spirit ye are not under the law (Galatians 5:18). The voluntary submission of believers to be led by the spirit is a choice that makes the law irrelevant. The moral life of Christians is governed by the fruit of the spirit, love, joy, peace, long-suffering, gentleness, goodness, faith, meekness, temperance; against such, there is no law. For more information, please reference Galatians 5:22-23. Obedience of this nature is known as holiness, righteousness, sanctification, and godliness. Thus, a behavioral devotion has been led by the Spirit, releasing us from the legal obligation to God's law.

Now we are delivered from the law. That being dead wherein we were held; that we should serve in newness of spirit and not in the oldness of the letter (Romans 7:6). Through Adam's sin, "Death, biological and spiritual, came to all men." A complex term that is "death" is a description of eternal alienation from God. Death is the consequence or repercussion for acts of "sin" and is the violation of standards established by God. Romans 6:23 states, "the wages of sin is death." The opposite of death is life. The decision to serve in the newness of the spirit and commit ourselves to Jehovah unites the believer entirely to Jesus. We are baptized into his death, resurrection and share the reward of everlasting life and reconciliation with God.

The purpose of the law to sanction God's will was to "teach, direct and instruct" as the authoritative rule of conduct and divine standards. The law is holy, just, and good (Romans 7:12, 13). The law was an instrument that makes us aware of the reality of our death. It is a system of choice to reject sin and choose righteousness. According to Romans 7:14, the law is spiritual and is the spiritual forerunner leading us to Christ. The analogy "You can lead a horse to water, but you cannot make him drink" describes the power of man's sinful nature and its impact on life-shaping choices: especially the most essential one, holiness or hell. Human weakness and ignorance imprisons us, and we become slaves to sin and continue to serve in the oldness of the letter. The Apostle Paul understood his struggles with indwelling sin and its relationship to the law. He was well aware of the battle for his mind, the antagonists' Christ and Satan. Choose your master.

Neither yield ye your members as instruments of unrighteousness unto sin, but yield yourselves unto God as those that are alive from the dead and your members as instruments of righteousness unto God (Romans 6:13). Christ is the choice to rescue us from ourselves and deliver us from the law. We are dead to sin by being baptized into Christ Jesus and His death, as the Glory of Jehovah raised Christ from death, hell, and the grave. We also have been resurrected to the newness of life, the old self crucified. The body of sin is done away with. We are "alive to God in Christ Jesus our Lord." No longer slaves to sin's advantage in the law. o wretched man that I am who will deliver me from this body of death (Romans 7:24).

The last enemy that shall be abolished or reduced to inactivity is death (1 Corinthians 15:26).

The law cannot save us from sin, producing death. Wherefore the law was our schoolmaster to bring us unto Christ, that we might be justified by faith. But after that faith is come, we are no longer under a schoolmaster (Galatians 3: 24-25). The law as a schoolmaster was our tutor, privately instructing righteousness. Education has different levels, and the goal is to graduate to the next level. The law is equivalent to high school education. The diploma achieved is faith which is the belief and confidence in God's plan of salvation through Jesus Christ. Justify means to be just, right or valid, to declare guiltless. We are justified by our faith. As gradation is the release from high school, the attainment of faith is the release from the law. For the next level of your education, the Holy Ghost will be your teacher but the comforter, which is the Holy Ghost whom the Father will send in my name, He shall teach you all things (John 14:26}. The degree and academic title that you will receive is a servant. There will be no diploma to document the graduation, only a crown of Glory. And when the chief shepherd shall appear, ye shall receive a crown of glory that fadeth not away (1 Peter 5:4). His Lord said unto him, well done, good and faithful servant; thou hast been faithful over a few things, I will make thee ruler over many things. Enter thou into the joy of thy Lord (Matthews 25:23). And by Him all that believe are justified from all things, from which ye could not be justified by the Law of Moses (Acts 13:39).

The emphasis of this text is the law of Moses cannot save the sinner. Only Christ's shed blood as a sacrifice made to God for the remission of our sins can justify the believer. For this is my blood of the New Testament, which is shed for many for the remission of sins (Matthew 26:28). And almost all things are by the law purged with blood; and without shedding of blood is no remission (Hebrews 9:22).

Legalism alone was not sufficient for remission. The law required almost everything to be purged with blood. Christ's blood was not only shed for the remission of sin. It was a method of ratifying the new covenant. When the new covenant became official, the law ended. For Christ is the end of the law for righteousness to every one that believeth (Romans 10:4).

Self-righteousness is an achievement of works. God's righteousness is granted to saints through faith in Christ. But wilt thou know, o vain man, that faith without works is dead? (James 2:20). Knowing that a man is not justified by the works of the law, but by the faith of Jesus Christ even we have believed in Jesus Christ, that we might be justified by the faith of Christ and not by the works of the law shall no flesh be justified (Galatians 2:16). Therefore we conclude that a man is justified by faith without the deeds of the law (Romans 3:28}. Even as David also describeth the blessedness of the man unto whom God imputeth righteousness without works (Romans 4:6). Not by works of righteousness which we have done, but according to His mercy, He saves us, by the washing of regeneration and renewing of the Holy Ghost, which He shed on us abundantly through Jesus Christ our savior (Titus 3:5-6). This only would I learn of you, received ye the spirit by the works of the law, or by the hearing of faith? (Galatians 3:2). Is the law then against the promises of God? God forbid; for if there had been a law given which could have given, life, verily righteousness should have been by the law. But the scripture hath concluded all under sin that the promise by faith of Jesus Christ might be given to them that believe.

Before faith came, we were kept under the law and shut up unto the faith, which should afterwards be revealed. Wherefore the law was our schoolmaster to bring us unto Christ, that we might be justified by faith. But after that faith has come, we are no longer under a schoolmaster, for ye are all children of God by faith in Christ Jesus (Galatians 3:21-26). The intended goal of the law was to unveil sin. The completion of this process was superseded by faith in Christ as the only way to obtain righteousness. That if thou shalt confess with thy mouth the Lord Jesus and shalt believe in thine heart that God hath raised him from the dead, thou shalt be saved. For with the heart, man believeth unto righteousness; and with the mouth, confession is made unto salvation (Romans 10:9-10).

Faith is one of the fundamental creeds of Christendom. A radical and total self-commitment to God's offer in Christ can save the sinner from being eternally lost. For this reason, the redemptive work of Christ on the cross at calvary is the logical end of the law. Christ hath redeemed us from the curse of the law, being made a curse for us;

for it is written, cursed is every one that hangeth on a tree (Galatians 3:13). But when the fullness of the time was come, God sent forth His Son made of a woman and made under the law. To redeem them that were under the law that we might receive the adoption of sons (Galatians 4:4-5). Having abolished in His flesh the enmity, even of commandments contained in ordinances; for to make in Himself of twain one new man, so making peace (Ephesians 2:15). For the priesthood being changed, there is made of necessity a change also of the law (Hebrews 7:12). But now the righteousness of God without the law is manifested being witnessed by the law and the prophets (Romans 3:21). After much prayer and petitioning the Holy Spirit for wisdom, knowledge, and understanding of the subject matter, the Mosaic Law. By studying and cross-referencing scriptures, mediation on words and clarifying meanings, a comprehensive survey of the topic's application, explanation, and illustration comprehending the weather of the theological truth, I have concluded the Bible makes it clear by the "harmony of The

Gospels" that the Mosaic Law is abolished through the death and resurrection of Jesus Christ our Lord. o Death, where is thy sting? o grave, where is thy victory? The sting of death is sin; and the strength of sin is the law. Therefore, we conclude that a man is justified by faith without the deeds of the law (Romans 3:28).

But thanks be to God which giveth us the victory through our Lord Jesus Christ (1 Corinthians 15: 55-57). Having been set free from the law of sin and death, Christians from and after 33 A.D. became part of a new spiritual priesthood that is not supported by tithes. As Christians, they were encouraged to give support to the Christian ministry both by their own ministerial activity and by material contributions, instead of giving fixed, specified, or mandatory amounts; they were to contribute "according to what a person has" giving as they resolved in their heart, not grudgingly.

But this I say, he which soweth sparingly shall reap also sparingly and he which soweth bountifully shall reap also bountifully. Every man according as he purposeth in his heart, so let him give: not grudgingly or necessity for God loveth a cheerful giver (2 Corinthians 9: 6-7). And there came a certain poor widow, and she threw in two mites, which make a farthing; and he called unto them, verily I say unto you, that this poor widow hath cast more in, than all they which have cast into the treasury: for all they did cast in of their abundance; but she of her want did cast in all that she had even all her living (Mark 12: 42-44). He that hath pity upon the poor lendeth unto the Lord and that which he that given will he pay him again (Proverbs 19:17). He that hath a bountiful eye shall be blessed; for he giveth of his bread to the poor (Proverbs 22:9). Christian stewardship calls for wise and responsible use of one's God-given resources. It involves faithfulness in using one's time, talents, and money. This is a type of New Testament sacrifice; an offering made to Jehovah to gain favor or show respect, to atone for transgression against God. They are not insincere acts, with alternative motives of manipulating God, with a prosperity seed harvest formula, constructed from Bible scriptures as a way to build wealth! But seek ye first the Kingdom of God and his righteousness; and all these things shall be added unto you (Matthew 6:33).

Believers, who participate in the building of God's Kingdom, will be blessed by God. Well done good and faithful over a few things. I will make thee ruler over many things; enter thou into the joy of thy Lord (Matthew 25: 23). The best formula for contribution to the church is what Paul ordered to the churches of Galatia and Corinth for the collections of funds to aid the Jerusalem church. His instructions are a New Testament philosophy of giving, a substitute for the Old Testament principle of tithing. Upon the first day of the week, let every one of you lay by him in store as God that prospered him, that there be no gatherings when I come (1 Corinthians 16:2). The concept in this text is a freewill offering, "From what you have" while in prosperity or bankruptcy. Cheerful spirit-led giving, subordinating to the authority of God's New Testament covenant.

This eternal principle of giving is the foundation of my theology, a doctrine that contradicts the false teaching and misinterpretations of storehouse tithing mandated custom of the Old Testament for the purpose of up-keeping an earthly sanctuary and a priesthood inferior to Christ's storehouse tithe.

One-tenths of a person's income is presented as an offering to God, the owner of the Promised Land.

According to Deuteronomy 26:2, ten percent of the crops produced by the land were paid to support the nation's priesthood and temple and used as a welfare system for the poor. Numbers 18:1-20 tells us of the provisions God made for the Priests and Levites who were responsible for the security and upkeep of the temple. God gave tithes exclusively to the Levites because they had no inheritance in the land. The Levites gave a tenth of what they received to the Aaronic Priesthood for their support.

(Numbers 18:25-29). Tithes also consisted of the herds and flocks as part of the obligatory taxation. Concerning the tithes of the herd or the flock, even of whatsoever passeth under the rod. The tenth shall be holy unto the Lord (Leviticus 27:32).

The law of the tithe, Deuteronomy 14:24-26, says that if a person lives too far from the temple where all the tithes were paid, he could sell his tithe and use the money gained from the sale to purchase a substitute tithe when he arrived at the temple. And if the way be too long for thee, so that thou art not able to carry it; or if the place be too far from thee, which the Lord thy God shall choose to set His name there, when the Lord they God hath blessed thee; then shalt thou turn it into money, and bind up the money in thine hand and shalt go unto the place which the Lord thy God shall choose. And those shalt bestow that money for whatsoever they soul lusteth after, for oxen, or for sheep, or for wine, or for strong drink, or for whatsoever they soul desireth; and thou shalt eat there before the Lord thy God, and thou shalt rejoice, thou and thine household (Deuteronomy 14: 24-26).

Money changers set up at the temple, exchange the money for a substitute tithe, or exchange foreign currency for acceptable money to pay the temple tithe. The money changer charged a fee for each transaction, sacrificial animal sales for profits led to corrupt business and gross abuses that Jesus Christ condemned. And Jesus went into the temple of God and cast out all them that sold and bought in the temple and overthrew the tables of the money-changers and the seats of them that sold doves and said unto them, it is written My house shall be called The House of Prayer; but ye have made it a den of thieves (Matthew 21- 12-13). The money changers knew that substitute tithes were beneficial to Jews from distant lands because a penalty of 20 percent was added to the tithe if the Israelites used the money to tithe instead of the first fruit or the firstling of the flock. And if a man will at all redeem ought of his tithes, he shall add thereto the fifth part thereof (Leviticus 27:31).

Tithes did not apply to money but to grains, animals, and fowls to build up the temple storehouse. Money offerings were deposited in the treasury. Jesus sat over against the treasury and beheld how the people cast money into the treasury, and many that were rich cast in much (Mark 12:41). Jehovah placed moral imperative tithing laws were binding on Israel to keep the Levites and Priests from having to support themselves through secular work and consequently neglecting their religious obligation. When the people became disobedient and negligent of their responsibility to tithe, the priesthood suffered. New Testament churches in the year 2009 "Anno Domini" (A.D.), "Year of our Lord" suffer the same as the Aaronic priesthood of 1471Before Christ (B.C.) due to Biblical disobedience, two different paths of giving for the purpose of building Jehovah's Kingdom. The similarity of both eras was monetary selfishness. The problem then and today was the greed of people, excessively stockpiling the raw material of the land at the expense of others. This took place in 2008 A.D. during the Great Recession housing slump and the worst financial crisis in 70 years. The so-called "Subprime Mortgage Crisis." Also, during the COVID-19 pandemic of 2020 A.D., the church had left the building, and the hoarding of goods began!

The land of milk and honey itself was rich (Exodus 3:8, 17). The abundance of the promised land (Exodus 6:4) was a blessing from God to be shared by all the Israelites to ensure the welfare of the disadvantaged (Deuteronomy 14: 8, 29; 26:11). The priests and the Levites (2 Chronicles 31:4) Jehovah gave Israel tithing laws for this purpose.

Tithing laws were not excessive. God promised to prosper Israel for obeying by opening "the floodgates of Heaven." Opponents of tithing believe that there was no stated penalty for failing to tithe under the law. Proponents of tithing argue the modern-day teachings that the consequences and repercussion of disobedience to the tithing laws, a curse will be applied to the offender! Opportunities for blessings will be missed! According to Malachi 3:9, ye are cursed with a curse: for ye have robbed me, even this whole nation. Jehovah's pronouncing of this curse upon them who declined the summons to tithe was the legal punishment of the law covenant. Christians are redeemed from the curses of the Mosaic Law by the crucifixion of Christ. Galatians 3:10-13 states, *"For as many as are of the works of the law are under the curse: for it is written, Cursed is every one that continueth not in all things which are written in the book of the law to do them. 11But that no man is justified by the law in the sight of God, it is evident: for, The just shall live by faith. 12And the law is not of faith: but, The man that doeth them shall live in them. 13Christ hath redeemed us from the curse of the law, being made a curse for us: for it is written, Cursed is every one that hangeth on a tree:"* The Apostle Paul wrote in Ephesians 1:3, *"Blessed be the God and Father of our LORD Jesus Christ, who hath blessed us with all spiritual blessings in heavenly places in Christ:"*

God has blessed us by Christ in eternity past with every spiritual blessing retained in Heaven granted to the believer on earth as needed for Christian growth. We can be blessed by tithing and sacrificial offerings of the law covenant: If God honors ignorance that spiritually nullifies the Gospel's validity. The "blessings/cursing" prosperity theology doctrines that teach God blesses the tither and curses those who do not participate undermines faith in the precious blood of Jesus Christ. The most significant ransom paid the price, releasing us from the obligation of the law—deliverance from sin and death, reconciliation to God. We need not take the doctrine of man as fact. Let us look to the Bible, God's word, for in them, we will learn the facts about tithes. We often state that we believe the Bible to be the only infallible Word of God. Not the word of Brother Short or the many priests, Bishops, Elders, and Pastors. All doctrine must be able to stand up to the test of Bible truths. The scriptures must collaborate every church doctrine and every word spoken from the pulpit. According to 2 Timothy 3:16, all scripture is given by inspiration of God and is profitable for doctrine, for reproof, for correction, for instruction in righteousness. Acts 17:10-11 shows how the people in the city of Beroea preached the word of God by the Apostle Paul, and they received the word with open minds. And when Paul was finished preaching, they would check the scriptures to see if what he preached was Bible truth. They did not take Paul's word as the bottom line. They cross-referenced what he said against the scriptures.

I challenge everyone who reads what I write to hold it up to the test of the Bible and come to know the truth for themselves! Do not take my word as if it is infallible. I am amazed at the number of saints in the church for seven years and more who still need an understanding of John 3:16. Among them are doctors, lawyers, computer specialists, and businessmen and women, to name a few, who have mastered their potential in their fields of expertise, nevertheless are still babes in Christ. 1 Corinthians 3:1-2, And I brethren, could not speak unto you as unto spiritual, but as unto carnal, even as unto babes in Christ. I have fed you with milk and not with meat; for hitherto ye were not able to bear it, neither yet now are ye able. Hebrews 5:13-14 states, for Every one that useth milk is unskillful in the word of righteousness; for he is a babe. But strong meat belongeth to them that are of full even those who by reason of use have their sense exercised to discern both good and evil. This book, for some, will be strong meat. But it is necessary to teach, preach and learn accurate knowledge of the Bible. There is no higher activity for the mind than to seek to know the Creator!

My Bible tells me to grow in grace and the knowledge of our Lord and Savior Jesus Christ (2 Peter 3:18). Grow in Knowledge! We all started as babes in Christ, and as long as we remain babes, the hand that is rocking the cradle is that of the devil. Satan has accurate knowledge of the Bible. He knows that it reveals his plans for deceiving the saints. Study to show thyself approved unto God, a workman that needeth not to be ashamed, rightly dividing the word of truth (2 Timothy 2:15). I am an education advocate for Bible truth, reformation principles of interpretation. But thou, O Daniel, shut up the words and seal the book, even to the time of the end. Many shall run to and fro and knowledge shall be increased (Daniel 12:4). The significance of this scripture is God indicated our understanding is an evolutionary process, and for this reason, the Holy Ghost teaches those who seek spiritual growth.

But the comforters, which is the Holy Ghost, whom the Father will send in my name, He shall teach you all things (John 14:26). Which things also we speak, not in the words which man's wisdom teacheth, but which the Holy Ghost teacheth; comparing spiritual things with spiritual (1 Corinthians 2:13).

Pastors train for many years in seminary, the quest for homiletical theory, discovering improved methods, and fresh principles to study the Bible. A thorough, practical examinant an investigation of history, prophecy, human psychology, social development, and motivational concepts. One day graduating from the institution with human intellect textbook interpretations, "exposition," and "exegesis" of carnal minds. Educated fools, thousands of dollars spent on achievement, accomplishments of evangelical intelligence that could have been attained by petition addressed to the Holy Ghost to open the hidden treasures of God's wisdom for free, no charge or tuition. If any of you lack wisdom, let him ask of God that giveth to all men liberally and upbraideth not: and it shall be given you; seek, and ye shall find; knock, and it shall be opened unto you (Matthew 7:7). It is not my intent to belittle theological seminaries or insult the students who earnestly attend in response to the divine call of God. One of the ultimate purposes of this publisher is to expostulate the false prophets scholar that intellectualizes scripture, purports Holiness, utilize their acquired knowledge to extort God's "Chosen Generation." For I know that after my departing shall grievous wolves enter in among you, not sparing the flock (Acts 20:29). For there shall arise false Christs, and false prophets and shall show great sign and wonders; in so much that if it were possible they shall deceived the very elect (Matthew 24:24).

The main deception scheme perpetrated is conducted from the church pulpit. For we wrestle not against flesh and blood, but against principalities against powers, against the rulers of the darkness of this world, against spiritual wickedness in high places (Ephesians 6:12). The perspective view from seated in the pew, the elevated pulpit is a high place, where self-serving money worshipers have infiltrated among the faithful and true prophets, preaching as an occupation. The actions of these hustlers have left many tithing storehouses empty. If tithing benefited the needy saints as God originally purposed, no Christian believer would have to request Government Welfare with the current economic crisis. Instead, the church tithe is used to pay the mortgage debts from building multi-million dollar cathedrals, and their storehouses are empty. "The handwriting is on the wall" mene, mene, tekel, upharsin. You have been weighed and measured number and found wanting {Daniel 5: 25-26). Tithing is the primary source of funds for many local churches. Money is needed for church business. The electric and gas bill must be paid.

For this reason, the tithe contributor does not challenge the fact that there is no meat in the House of the Lord. The tithe teachers manipulate the truth because they do not trust your willingness to give {Malachi 3:6-10) is emphasized before the offering is collected. The recital of the tithe law is a classical conditioning stimulus technique used to evoke emotional responses to produce positive attitudes toward tithing. Repeatedly presented tithing becomes a learned conscious behavior. Will a man rob God? Yet ye have robbed me. But ye say where in have we robbed thee? In tithes and offerings (Malachi 3:8).

This text gets your attention. The negative reinforcement of you visualizing yourself, holding Jesus at gunpoint, causes interpersonal conviction derived from moral reasoning. Bring ye all tithes into the storehouse, that there may be meat in mine house, and prove now therewith, saith the Lord of Host. If I will not open you the windows of Heaven and pour you out a blessing that there shall not be room enough to receive it (Malachi 3:10). The poured blessing of Malachi 3:10 is the reward for being obedient. It is a form of positive reinforcement. The word "blessing" has emotional connotations that make you feel good about paying tithes. As a spontaneous secondary positive reinforcement for more immediate gratification, the worship choir sings an uplifting selection. Timely schedules of conditioning religious ritualism can result in the brainwashing of some believers. For I am the Lord I change not: Therefore ye sons of Jacob are not consumed (Malachi 3:6). Going on the premise that God never changes to justify Old Testament requirements as practices about contemporary sanctification is hypocritical because of the change in how and what we tithe. If God is the same yesterday, today, and forever, theocracies teach but do not practice what they preach. The inconsistencies of tithe customs comparing Old Testament principles to discrepancies applied today imply the implausible contradiction that God has changed. Money takes the place of the first fruits. Tithes are to be collected weekly, not yearly. The orphans and widows can fend for themselves. The empty storehouse is acceptable. Strange but Hallelujah anyhow!

It is my testimony that not all of God's storehouses are empty. When the steel mill I worked at closed and I became unemployed, my financial resources depleted and Saint Mary's Roman Catholic Church provided assistance. As an act of gratitude, I will donate a portion of the proceeds from this book to St. Mary's Church to help continue their ministry. For St. Mary's Church to give aid to others, someone had to make an offering or pay their tithes. This sacrifice is beneficial to the church and mankind worldwide.

Moreover, the monetary gift given by the assembly keeps the church from extinction. For this reason, I do not wish to discourage having good spirits when sacrificing the fruit of your labor, giving thanks to building Jehovah's kingdom. Imagine this present world without the church of God. The insight of truth pertaining to the sacred writing of the Bible causes controversy between followers of the Old Testament law and Holy Spirit-led intentions of the New Testament believers. All scripture is given by inspiration of God and is profitable for doctrine for instruction in righteousness (2 Timothy 3:16}.

When comparing scripture with scripture, understanding the purpose of the Old and New Testaments is a prerequisite for discerning the truth. The Old Testament is composed of 39 books of history, law, poetry, major and minor prophets, and wisdom. They begin with God's creation of the world and end with prophecies that point to the Messiah's coming and establishing a new covenant. Who hath believed our report? and to whom is the arm of the Lord revealed? For he shall grow up before Him as a tender plant, and as a root out of dry ground. He hath no form nor comeliness and when we shall see him there is no beauty that we should desire him. He is despised and rejected of men; a man of sorrows and acquainted with grief and we hid as it were our faces from him; he was despised and we esteemed him not. Surely he hath borne our griefs and carried our sorrow yet we did esteem him stricken smitten of God and afflicted. But he was wounded for our transgressions he was bruised for our Iniquities. The chastisement of our peace was upon him and with his stripes we are healed. All we like sheep have gone astray; we have turned everyone to his own way and the Lord that laid on him the iniquity of us all. He was oppressed and he was afflicted yet he opened not his mouth. He is brought as a lamb to the slaughter and as a sheep before her shearers is dumb so he openeth not his mouth. He was taken from prison and from judgment and who sh_all declare his generation? For he was cut off out of the land of the living; for the transgression of my people was he stricken. And he made his grave with the wicked and with the rich in his death because he had done no violence neither was any deceit in his mouth.

Yet it pleased the Lord to bruise him. He hath put him to grief. When thou shalt make his soul an offering for sin, he shall see his seed. He shall prolong his days and the pleasure of the Lord shall prosper in his hand. He shall see of the travail of his soul and shall be satisfied by his knowledge shall my righteous servant justify many; for he shall bear their iniquities. Therefore, will I divide him a portion with the great and he shall divide the spoil with the strong; because he hath poured out his soul unto death; and he was numbered with the transgressors and he bares the sin of many and made intercession for the transgressors (Isaiah 53: 1-12).

Jesus Christ is the central figure in these passages, not Muhammad. Christ is pictured in the Old Testament; He is the theme of it. Starting in the book of Genesis 3:14-15, Christ was the seed of the woman. In the book of Exodus 12: 1-11, Christ was pictured as the Passover lamb. The book of Psalm 22:1-3 foretold of Christ on the Cross. There are more scriptures to illustrate the Old Testament representation of Jesus Christ. By featuring Christ, it brings into focus the New Testament. Jesus' reference to "the New Testament in my blood" in 1 Corinthians @'.1.1:2 5 unifies Christ and the new dispensation as one. Think beyond human intellect and connect the spiritual dots of the scriptures.

Behold the days come, saith the Lord, that I will make a new covenant with the House of Israel and with the House of Judah (Jeremiah 31: 31). This prophecy foresees the new covenant that is symbolic of Jesus Christ; they're inseparable. Connect the dots. Able's sacrifice pictured the slain savior. Connect the dots. Abraham rejoiced to see the coming day of Christ. Connect the dots. David knew of the coming savior. Connect the dots. Isaiah knew about the virgin birth. Connect the dots. Daniel told of the coming king of the Jews. Connect the dots. Michah wrote that Bethlehem would be the place where the savior is born. Connect the dots. Zecharia described the wounds in his hands and declared all should look on him whom they pierced. Connect the dots. Job knew that his redeemer lives. Connect the dots. The culmination of all the connected dots is the Old Testament bore witness to Christ and revealed the New Testament that ultimately unveiled the Glory of the Old Testament.

CHAPTER 2
THE LAW

And it came to pass, when Moses came down from Mount Sinai with the two tables of the testimony in Moses' hand. When he came down from the mount, that Moses wist not that the skin of his face shone while he talked with him. And when Aaron and all the children of Israel saw Moses, behold the skin of his face shone; and they were afraid to come nigh him. And Moses called unto them and Aaron and all the rulers of the congregation returned unto him; and Moses talked with them. And afterward all the Children of Israel came nigh; and he gave them in commandment all that the Lord had spoken with him in Mount

Sinai. And until Moses had done speaking with them, he put a veil on his face. But when Moses went in before the Lord to speak with him he took the veil off, until he came out.

And he came out, and spake unto the children of Israel that which he was commanded. And the children of Israel saw the face of Moses, that the skin of Moses' face shone: and Moses put the vail upon his face again until he went in to speak with him. (Exodus 34:29-35). The veil concealed the radiance of God's Glory, which typified the Old Testament's majestic revelation that the Israelites could not see, symbolizing their spiritual blindness and ignorance about Christ, a stumbling block for the Jews, unfortunately.

And not as Moses, which put a veil over his face, that the children of Israel could not steadfastly look to the end of that which is abolished. But their minds were blinded; for until this day remaineth the same veil untaken away in the reading of the Old Testament; which veil is done away in Christ. But even unto this day when Moses is read the veil is upon their heart (2 Corinthians 3:13-15). The veil that Moses wore hid vital truths of a relationship with God. Similar to the veil of the temple that separated the Holy of Holies, the sanctuary of God's very presence. Both veils restrict the direct access to God and comprehension of his plan of salvation in Christ alone. And Jesus cried with a loud voice and gave up the ghost. And the veil of the temple was rent in twain from the top to the bottom (Mark 15:37-38).

Tearing of the veil indicates free access for all to God, made possible by Christ's crucifixion. A proper relationship with God for both Jews-- and Gentiles reformed "one new man" the Christian church. The hostility between the two groups came from misconstruing the purpose of the Mosaic Law and exalting themselves as superior to Gentiles. Christ abolished this enmity by removing the Mosaic Law, which was the middle wall of partition.

For he is our peace. Who hath made both one, and hath broken down the middle wall of partition between us; having abolished in his flesh the enmity, even the Law of

Commandments contained in ordinances; for to make in himself of twain one new man, so making peace (Ephesians 2:1). The nullification of the law served as the common denominator evenly dividing God's grace between Jews and Gentiles, an influential act for the probability of Harmony. Amid the two groups, as harmonious as the Old and New Testament. Jesus commented on the law and the meaning of abolished. Think not that I am come to destroy the law, or the prophets; I have not come to destroy, but to fulfill. For verily I say unto you, until Heaven and earth pass, one jot or one tittle shall in no wise pass from the law, until all be fulfilled (Matthew 5:17-18). Jesus states that he came to fulfill the law·. This means he came to convert the law into actuality by compliance to satisfy entirely every detailed instruction contained in the Old Testament law. He carried out the promised desire expected prophecies of the Messiah, literally bringing about completion, an end of the law. This achievement of perfection Christ the fulfiller accomplishes by His death and resurrection.

Until differing interpretations of eschatology result concludes, the advent of Christ was the beginning of the nullification of the Old Testament ceremonial system, and his sacrificial death was fulfilling divine purpose. Without realizing these essential facts, understanding Jesus' allegiance to the Old Testament law is difficult. Intelligent comprehension of scriptures is not incomplete. Jesus rightly understood Mosaic Code principles and precepts. His compliance was the fulfillment of Old Testament prophecies. Theoretically, Jesus was under the law. God's grace abounds, and Christ superseded at the time of His resurrection; until then, the law was in effect. Woe unto you scribes and Pharisees, hypocrites! For ye pay tithe of mint and anise and cumin, and have omitted the weightier matters of the law, judgment, mercy and faith; these ought ye to have done, and not to leave the other undone (Matthew 23:23). Tithe teachers use this text to prove that we should pay tithes.

Jesus told the Scribes and Pharisees, "These ought ye to have done." Jesus tells them to pay tithes because the law was still in effect.

Tithe teacher in the big picture, your evidence is invalid because it is fragmentary and lacks the totality of references to parallel passages on the subject of tithing, the ensample of the written statement of character. Hebrews chapter seven necessitates removing the Mosaic Law because the Aaronic Priesthood changed to the superlative priesthood of Christ. The Aaronic priesthood and Mosaic Law are inextricably bound. The passing of the Levitical priesthood abolished every ordinance pertaining to that priesthood, including tithing laws contextually by the context Hebrews chapter seven. It is illogical to teach that the disannulling of the Commandment excludes tithing. To indoctrinate this belief negates Paul's teachings concerning the Mosaic legal system (2 Corinthians 3:7-11; Galatians 3:9-25; Romans 7:1-6, 10:4). The Bible tells us as saints to worship in spirit and in truth (John 4:24).

The truth about paying tithes in the New Testament church is not under the law, but it is under grace. Tithes are a part of the law. I am speaking of the Mosaic Law that came into existence when God constituted Moses mediator of the Law covenant with Israel. This covenant is known as the Old Covenant. A covenant is an agreement between two people based on mutual promises people make to each other. Has the Old Covenant or law been abolished? Hebrews 8:6-13 tells us there is fault with the Old Covenant, and a New Covenant is needed. What was wrong with the Old Covenant according to Hebrews 8:6-13? Hebrews 8:6 says that the old covenant required better promises. It had poor promises; therefore, a new covenant was established on better promises.

Hebrews 8:7 says the first covenant had faults in it. It was not perfect.

So let us look at the poor promises and the faults of the old covenant. According to Exodus 19:3-6, God is making a proposal to the people of Israel at Sinai. He suggests that they enter into an agreement if Israel keeps my covenant and follows my laws; I will bless the nation of Israel and make them my peculiar people. God sent Moses to present these promises to the people of Israel. These are the foundation for a covenant; promises make an agreement if they are expected. Exodus 20:19, The people respond to Moses by saying, "We will hear." They excepted the terms God had set in His laws.

So here are the old covenant promises made between God and the people of Israel. To make this covenant official, it had to be sealed with blood. Exodus 24:3-8, The covenant was sealed. The people made burnt offerings and sacrificed peace offerings of oxen unto the Lord. Exodus 24:6, Moses sprinkled half the blood onto the altar. The people promised to keep the law, and God promised to bless them if they would.

Was Israel obedient to God? No. The people had turned to idol worship and corrupted themselves only a few days after the covenant was made. Moses was in the mount forty days and forty nights. During this time, the people lost their obedience to the commandments of God. Now we can see the poor promises of the old covenant where promises were made and broken by the people of Israel. Hebrews 8:8-9 states, for finding fault with them, he saith behold, the days come, saith the Lord, when I will make a new covenant with the house of Isreal and with the house of Judah. Not according to the covenant that I made with their fathers in the day when I took them by the hand to lead them out of Egypt; because they continued not in my covenant and I regarded them not, saith the Lord. These verses show that it was the people who were at fault and their failure to keep the promises to obey God's law lead to the need for a new covenant.

What are the better promises of the new covenant? Hebrews 8:10, God says I will make a covenant, I will put my laws into their mind and write them in their hearts; and I will be to them a God. Notice in these verses God says I will be, I will make, I will put. Can you see who is making all the promises? God is making all the promises this is why the new covenant is based on better promises. The old covenant was based on the people of Israel, their weakness, and the promise that they would keep the laws with human effort and strength. The most significant difference between these two covenants is the old covenant was made official by the blood of animal sacrifices. The new covenant is sealed and made official by the blood of Jesus (Hebrews 13:20-21). Testament is the same word as a covenant. Notice how Hebrews 9:16-17 uses the word testament in place of covenant. Hebrews 9:17 states, a testament is of force after men are dead. It is of no strength while the testator lives. Hebrews 9:16 states, for where a testament is, there must also of necessity be the death of the testator.

CHAPTER 3
GRACE OR DISGRACE

Grace or Disgrace

Jesus Christ, the testator of the new covenant. Hebrews 10:4 states for it is not possible that the blood of bulls and goats should take away sins. Hebrews 9:22 and almost all things are by the law purged with blood; and without shedding of blood is no remission. Hebrews 10:9-10, then said he, lo, I come to do thy will, o God. He taketh away the first that he may establish the second. By which will we are sanctified through the offering of the body of Jesus Christ once for all. Hebrews 10:12 states, but this man, after he had offered one sacrifice for sins forever, sat down on the right hand of God.

Matthews 5:17-18 states, this sacrifice by Jesus Christ fulfilled the law and set aside the old covenant and establishes a new covenant and the foundation of new. Grace is the kindness of a master toward a slave. Thus by analogy, it has come to signify the kindness of God to man undeserving thereof. Grace is the concept of kindness bestowed upon someone undeserving favor, such as sinners. According to Ephesians 2:4-5, but God, who is rich in mercy, for His great love wherewith He loved us, even when we were dead in sins hath quickened us together with Christ by grace ye are saved. In John 1:17, for the law was given by Moses, but grace and truth came by Jesus Christ. In Galatians 2:21, I do not frustrate the grace of God for if righteousness comes by the law, then Christ is dead in vain.

The law of Moses consists of more than 600 individual laws or commandments, including the Ten Commandments, tithe laws, and the law to keep a weekly Sabbath. God inspired the Apostle Paul to write Romans 7:7. I had not known sin but by the law; for I had not known lust, except the law had said, thou shalt not covet. This is a direct reference to the Ten Commandments. Another example is written in Colossians 2:16. Let no man, therefore, judge you in meat or in drink or in respect of an holy day or of the new moon or of the Sabbath days. Notice in this verse Paul did not exclude the Sabbath, one of the Ten Commandments (Romans 14:5 and Galatians 4:9-10). I like this scripture because, to me, it resolves the issue about eating pork! Let no man, therefore, judge you in meat. This means the food that you eat does not affect a person's salvation. Nevertheless, for health reasons that are well documented by science and the Bible, bless your food, give thanks to the Lord, eat what you want in moderation, and exercise regularly!

Because of how we are fed, our spiritual diet being The Word of God, many of the saints could use a good laxative to flush out the untruths and false teachings. Many of the New Testament saints have a smorgasbord theology similar to a buffet meal with a variety of food to choose from. You cannot pick and choose from the word of God what you want to be fed. In 1 Peter 5:1-3, the elders which are among you I exult, who am also an Elder, and witness of the sufferings of Christ and also a partaker of the Glory that shall be revealed. Feed the flock of God which is among you, taking the oversight thereof, not by constraint, but willingly; not for filthy lucre, but of a ready mind; neither as being Lords over God's heritage being ensamples to the flock.

Jeremiah 3:15, And I will give you pastors according to mine heart, which shall feed you with knowledge and understanding. Acts 20:28 states, Take heed therefore unto yourselves and to all the flock over thee which the Holy Ghost hath made you overseers, to feed the Church of God, which He hath purchased with his own blood. In John 21:15-17, Jesus saith to Simon Peter feed my sheep! The Bible is much like the owner's manual of a car. Follow the guidelines and instructions carefully and you will receive the maximum performance and life expectancy of the automobile. The Bible is man's manual to living a Holy life and receive abundant life here on Earth, leading to everlasting life with our Father in Heaven. Do you believe we can get to Heaven following the instructions of a smorgasbord mentality of some of the Elders who pick and choose what they preach out of God's word, to their own advantage for filthy lucre? The elders feed you the verses from Malachi 3:10, which states Bring ye all the tithes into the storehouse, but they will not feed you the Bible the fact that the law of the tithes was ceremonially abolished in Christ (Hebrews 7:18; 8:13; 10:1; 12:27). The elders walk down the buffet line and pick what they want to feed the congregation. They will serve you a large plate of salvation with some repentance and righteousness, fatten you up with holiness, then slip you some tithes for dessert!

What's wrong with this picture? On that same buffet line right next to tithes was the Sabbath, but they skipped over that because the scriptures say that it is no longer binding to the church today! God has done away with one of His top ten laws, the Sabbath, written with His own fingers as a memorial to His creation, but he did not change the laws of tithes! Pastors, be careful what you preach. For even the carnal-minded do not need any light to see the deceitful utterances you speak.

And we wonder why the pews of the church are empty! The Elders and the Scribes during the time of Stephen knew the fact that Jesus would change the customs which Moses delivered. But you modern-day Pharisees do not feed the flock of God the all-important knowledge of the fact that the law is abolished and the grace of God released us from the duty of the law by providing a replacement, a new covenant of love.

Romans 5:21, That as sin hath reigned unto death, even so might grace reign through righteousness unto eternal life by Jesus Christ our Lord. Romans 6:15, What then shall we sin because we are not under the law, but under grace? God forbid. Grace is similar to a pardon meaning to forgive someone for an offense! For example, let's say a man committed the crime of murder, and the judge sentenced him to death by the electric chair. The man then appeals to the Governor and receives a pardon. The execution is canceled, and the man is set free! Now that he has a pardon from the Governor, can he break the law by running a red light or stealing from the supermarket? No. He must still keep the law. Now it appears I have contradicted all that I have expressed by saying he must keep the law. It is unimportant to distinguish the difference between moral laws and ceremonial laws. God's moral laws could never be abolished. If you removed them, the world would be in a state of chaos, turmoil, confusion, and disarray. It would be like removing the law of gravity. Everything would become weightless and float in space. Moral laws are not a part of the Law of Moses. They were in existence before the time when Moses received the Commandments at Mount Sinai.

In the beginning, was the temptation of Adam (Genesis 2:17) but of the Tree of Knowledge of Good and Evil, thou shalt not eat of it for in the day that thou eatest thereof thou shalt surely die. This is a law of obedience to God. Another example is when Cain killed his brother Abel, and Cain said unto the Lord, my punishment is greater than I can bear (Genesis 4:13). How can you punish Cain if there was no moral law not to kill? Then there was the wickedness of man during the days of Noah. It was the moral laws of God that set the standards for judgment. As for Sodom and Gomorrah's destruction, God's very same moral laws became their downfall. Ceremonial laws are sacrifice laws, circumcision laws, and the many laws handed down through Moses.

The divine principles of the Mosaic Laws are still of great value. By studying them, we learn about God and His purpose for man. Laws that apply to the New Testament church are:

>*Matthews 4:10, 1 Corinthians 10:20-22; 1 John 5:21;*
>*1 Corinthians 10:14; Matthew 6:9;*
>*Ephesians 6:1-2;*
>*Revelations 21:8; 1 John 3:15;*
>*Hebrews 13:4; Hebrews 8:7-13;*
>*Luke 22:20; Hebrews 13:1-25; 1 Thessalonians 4:3-7;*
>*Ephesians 4:25, 28; 1 Corinthians 6:9-11; Luke 12:15;*
>*Colossians 3:5; 1 John 5:3; Romans 13:8-10; Galatians 5:13,14;*
>*Matthews 22:36-40; John 13:34-35;*
>*Galatians 6:2;*

Hebrews 4:10; 1 Corinthians 16:2.

After studying these scriptures, have you noticed that many of the Old Covenant laws and principles were adopted into Christianity?

CHAPTER 4

WILL A MAN ROB GOD?

Will a Man Rob God?

Will a man rob God? Yet ye have robbed me but ye say wherein have we robbed thee? In my mind, if I can hear God say Ye have robbed me by robbing my flock of truth and knowledge of me and my holy scriptures! There is a tribe robbing God by robbing the man and woman of God, and this tribe is not the tribe of Levi. It is the tribe of modern-day Scribes and Pharisees preaching to the flock a doctrine of deception filled with theories. A few words of scripture are separated from the context to show its meaning to be exactly opposite to the interpretation intended by the Prophets or Apostles. Paul's farewell to Ephesus (Acts 20:28-30) take heed therefore unto yourselves, and to all the flock, over thee which the Holy Ghost hath made you overseers to feed the Church of God, which he hath purchased with his own blood. For I know this, that after my departing shall grievous wolves enter in among you. Not sparing the flock. Also, of your own selves shall men arise, speaking perverse things to draw away disciples after them. O Lord only if Moses, Daniel, Isaiah, Paul or Peter were here in this present world to set the record straight on such disjointed passages being perverted and used in the proof of doctrines that have no foundation in the word of God, robbing the sheep instead of feeding them the truth because the tithe is what keeps the church afloat. It pays the bills. The pastor fears that if the congregation comes into the knowledge that the law of tithing has been done away with, they will not give as much. Jehovah's Witnesses encourage the congregation to support the Christian ministry by giving what a person has resolved in his heart. They do not pay tithes to defray congregational expenses; nevertheless, they build new kingdom halls all over the world and upkeep them on the principle of cheerful giving.

A little light of truth should be inspirational. I find it hard to present a positive influence while exposing the negative doctrines and rituals of the Christian church. Divine truth will prevail; that is the supernatural inspiration of the Holy Scriptures. God does not need me to sugarcoat the message to encourage his inspired word to have attached perfect inspiration, motivation, divine influence mentally or emotionally and spiritually. And for me, that utterance may be given unto me, that I may open my mouth boldly, to make known the mystery of the Gospel for which I am an ambassador in bonds; that therein I may speak boldly, as I ought to speak (Ephesians 6:19-20).

As an agent of Christ, these scriptures are my motto, to speak with courage and clarity. To walk in the forefathers' wisdom, reformers knowing no fear but the fear of Jehovah and acknowledging the light of truth when revealed by the Holy Spirit. I am responsible for a powerful message to revive the ignorant, radical is my nature, not perfect Christian character, humility and meekness are not my forte. I believe this human imperfection is the foundation of my calling to champion the literacy of the reformed. Pray that the task of this conviction does not turn to the personal, but to God be the Glory, and according to His instruction of the everlasting covenant, I will teach the eternal principles of salvation, purpose, Glory, inheritance, redemption, and love. Tithing is a material thing used to teach eternal principles. A tithe is not spiritual or eternal.

For this reason, it is not part of the new covenant. If you can understand the critical Biblical concepts of the law and its intricacies; Congratulations, you have challenged your mind, and with this knowledge, you are spiritually out of bondage. Free your mind so that the flesh will follow the Kingdom of Heaven that is within.

EPILOGUE

E zekiel 13

1 And the word of the Lord came unto me, saying,

2 Son of man, prophesy against the prophets of Israel that prophesy, and say thou unto them that prophesy out of their own hearts, Hear ye the word of the Lord;

3 Thus saith the Lord God; Woe unto the foolish prophets, that follow their own spirit, and have seen nothing!

4 O Israel, thy prophets are like the foxes in the deserts.

5 Ye have not gone up into the gaps, neither made up the hedge for the house of Israel to stand in the battle in the day of the Lord.

6 They have seen vanity and lying divination, saying, The Lord saith: and the Lord hath not sent them: and they have made others to hope that they would confirm the word.

7 Have ye not seen a vain vision, and have ye not spoken a lying divination, whereas ye say, The Lord saith it; albeit I have not spoken?

8 Therefore thus saith the Lord God; Because ye have spoken vanity, and seen lies, therefore, behold, I am against you, saith the Lord God.

9 And mine hand shall be upon the prophets that see vanity, and that divine lies: they shall not be in the assembly of my people, neither shall they be written in the writing of the house of Israel, neither shall they enter into the land of Israel; and ye shall know that I am the Lord God.

These scriptures have nothing to do with tithes. I believe they speak to the foolish Prophets, denounce the stupid Prophetesses, and serve as a warning to the motivational speaker who wants to be a pastor. Moreover, the Pimp turned pastor spewing a message of prosperity, wishful thinking, deceptive, empty falsehoods of delusive words, and lying saying "the Lord saith!" Fleecing the flock of God with a vision of untruths and divining a lie, prophesying a feel-good message of wealth out their own heart, walking after their own spirit for personal gain of a fist full of dollars, deceiving the intimate group of Jehovah's people holding them in spiritual bondage of the Law of tithing after the sovereign Lord Jehovah delivered them from the Law, through the death, burial & resurrection of Jesus Christ.

As the author of this book, I must be mindful of God's wrath, understand and realize the consequences and repercussions of misrepresenting his word.

To my Christian Brothers & Sisters, stay woke, be vigilant, watch and pray, Matt.

26:41. There will always be spiritual predators like Jim Jones, David Koresh, Warren Jeffs who prey on the vulnerability of the meekness of the saints until the sound of the trump 1Cor. 15:52 and beyond. They will continue to exploit the word. I would rather have one thousand souls saved and offering one dollar than burden ten with a tithe of one hundred.

www.ingramcontent.com/pod-product-compliance
Lightning Source LLC
Chambersburg PA
CBHW072039080526
44578CB00007B/492